AUGUST, 2017

Houston's Hurricane Harvey Floods

by Kevin Blake

Consultant: Jeffry Evans
Meteorologist in Charge
National Weather Service
Houston/Galveston, Texas

BEARPORT
PUBLISHING

New York, New York

Credits

Cover, © Scott Dalton/The New York Times/Redux Pictures; 4–5, © michelmond/Shutterstock; 5, © Andrea Smith; 6, © David J. Phillips/AP Images; 7T, © Andrea Smith; 7B, © Damir Sagolj/Reuters; 8, © Malcolm McClendon/UPI/Newscom; 9, © Karl Spencer/iStock; 11L, © Everett Collection/Alamy; 11R, © Bob Daemmrich/Alamy; 12, © Michael Ciaglo/Houston Chronicle/AP Images; 13T, © HCA Healthcare; 13B, © michelmond/Shutterstock; 14–15, © CBP Photo/Alamy; 15R, © US Coast Guard Photo/Alamy; 16, © David J. Phillip/AP Images; 17, © Sam Armanino; 18, © Michael Wyke/EPA-EFE/REX/Shutterstock; 19, © Carlo Allegri/Reuters; 20, © Song Qiong/Xinhua News Agency/Newscom; 21L, © William Bruso/Viral Hog; 21R, © 2018 Dallas Morning News, Inc.; 22, © Carlos Barria/TPX Images of the Day/Reuters; 23T, © Nick Oxford/Reuters; 23B, © F. Carter Smith/Polaris/Newscom; 24, © Tribune Content Agency LLC/Alamy; 25, © michelmond/Shutterstock; 26, © John Glaser/AP Images; 27, © Military Collection/Alamy; 28T, © Andrea Smith; 28B, © HCA Healthcare; 29T, © Sam Armanino; 29B, © F. Carter Smith/Polaris/Newscom; 31, © Tim Bingham/Dreamstime; 32, © TrongNguyen/Dreamstime.

Publisher: Kenn Goin
Senior Editor: Joyce Tavolacci
Creative Director: Spencer Brinker
Design: Dawn Beard Creative
Photo Researcher: Thomas Persano

Library of Congress Cataloging-in-Publication Data

Names: Blake, Kevin, 1978– author.
Title: Houston's Hurricane Harvey floods / by Kevin Blake ; consultant,
  Jeffry Evans, Meteorologist in Charge, National Weather Service,
  Houston/Galveston, Texas.
Other titles: Hurricane Harvey floods
Description: New York, New York : Bearport Publishing, [2019] | Series: Code
  red| Includes bibliographical references and
  index.
Identifiers: LCCN 2018009273 (print) | LCCN 2018011037 (ebook) |
ISBN 9781684027071 (ebook) | ISBN 9781684026616 (library)
Subjects: LCSH: Hurricane Harvey, 2017—Juvenile literature. |
  Hurricanes—Texas—Juvenile literature. | Floods—Texas—Houston—Juvenile
  literature. | Disaster relief—Texas—Houston—Juvenile literature. |
  Houston (Tex.)—History—21st century—Juvenile literature.
Classification: LCC QC945 (ebook) | LCC QC945 .B56 2018 (print) |
DDC 976.4/141—dc23
LC record available at https://lccn.loc.gov/2018009273

For more information, write to Bearport Publishing Company, Inc., 45 West 21st Street, Suite 3B, New York, New York 10010. Printed in the United States of America.

10 9 8 7 6 5 4 3 2 1

Contents

Trapped!

Andrea Smith was trapped, and she was about to give birth. It was August 27, 2017, and **Hurricane** Harvey raged outside her Houston, Texas, home. Storm water surrounded her apartment building. It flooded the cars parked on her street and **transformed** roads into rushing rivers.

Over 3 feet (1 m) of water surrounded Andrea's home.

Frantically, Andrea's husband, Greg, dialed 911 for help. He tried the **Coast Guard**, too. "I couldn't get through," Greg says. The couple decided there was no other choice—they would have to deliver their baby at home. Just then, Greg heard a loud rumbling sound outside.

Andrea and Greg Smith

Hurricane Harvey hit Houston and other parts of southeastern Texas on August 25, 2017. Over a period of seven days, it dumped more rain on Texas than any other storm in US history!

A Helping Hand

Greg looked out the window and saw a huge dump truck powering down his block. He walked outside into the rising water and waved his arms at the truck. "We're here for *you*!" the men inside the vehicle yelled. Little did Andrea and Greg know that their neighbors had found a dump truck and a team of firemen to help them!

A dump truck drives down a flooded Houston street.

Nearly 2 feet (0.6 m) of rain fell in some parts of Houston within the first 12 hours of the storm.

As the big truck pulled in front of Andrea and Greg's building, their neighbors came out of their homes. They linked arms to form a human chain from Andrea's door to the truck. Greg led his wife through the waist-deep water, holding on to his neighbors as they went. Soon, the soaked pair climbed onto the truck and sped off toward the hospital. A few hours later, Andrea gave birth to a healthy baby girl named Adrielle.

66 Moments like this are incredibly precious and remind me of all the good in the world. 99

–Molly Akers, a neighbor of Andrea and Greg Smith's

Baby Adrielle and her relieved parents

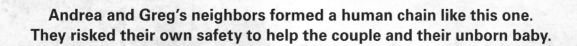

Andrea and Greg's neighbors formed a human chain like this one. They risked their own safety to help the couple and their unborn baby.

Massive Flooding

Hurricane Harvey's **torrential** rains left Andrea and Greg—along with millions of other Texans—in serious danger. The storm dropped over 33 trillion gallons (125 trillion l) of rain onto the state and surrounding area in five days. That's almost as much water as what travels over Niagara Falls in an entire year!

The rainwater was so heavy, it made a dent in the Earth's crust!

Cows stranded by the storm

Nearly 61 inches (155 cm) of rain fell near the city of Nederland, Texas. That amount set a new record for a single storm in the United States.

In a flat city like Houston, there's little place for that much water to drain. The city's **reservoirs** and sewers quickly overflowed, creating huge floods throughout the area. By the end of the storm, a space nearly the size of the state of New Jersey was underwater!

With approximately 6.5 million people, Houston is the fourth-largest city in the United States. Much of the area was flooded during the hurricane.

Super-Storm

On August 13, this powerful hurricane started as a small **tropical wave** in the Caribbean Sea, becoming a tropical storm four days later. As it traveled west toward the United States, it slowed down over the warm water in the Gulf of Mexico. Water over 80°F (27°C) produces **water vapor** that makes storms more powerful. This helped transform the small tropical storm into a forceful hurricane.

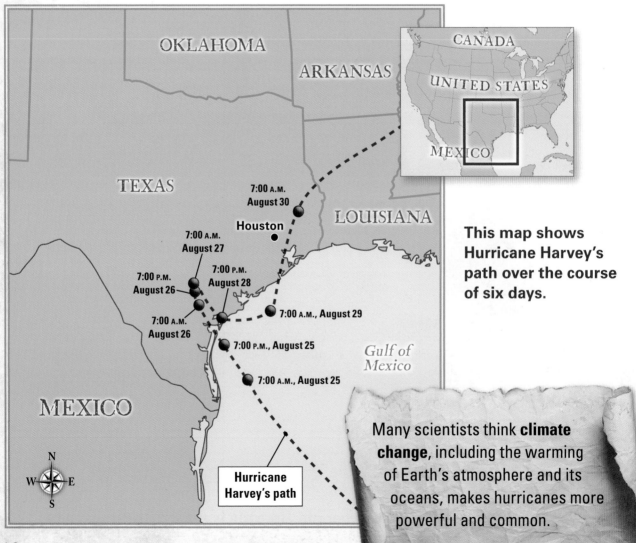

OKLAHOMA

ARKANSAS

CANADA

UNITED STATES

MEXICO

TEXAS

7:00 A.M.
August 30

LOUISIANA

Houston

7:00 A.M.
August 27

7:00 P.M.
August 26

7:00 P.M.
August 28

7:00 A.M.
August 26

7:00 A.M., August 29

7:00 P.M., August 25

Gulf of
Mexico

7:00 A.M., August 25

MEXICO

N
W E
S

Hurricane
Harvey's path

This map shows Hurricane Harvey's path over the course of six days.

Many scientists think **climate change**, including the warming of Earth's atmosphere and its oceans, makes hurricanes more powerful and common.

When scientists called **meteorologists** learned about the deadly storm, they warned people living in the hurricane's path about its dangers. Texas Governor Greg Abbott encouraged residents to **evacuate** before the storm hit. Many people were reluctant to leave their homes and businesses, though. They had a very difficult choice: stay and risk getting hurt or leave their beloved city?

Texas Governor Greg Abbott

A photograph of the storm taken by a satellite

A Brave Doctor

For many Texans who decided to stay home, including Dr. Stephen Kimmel, a **surgeon**, Hurricane Harvey would put their courage to the test. With floodwaters swirling around his house, Dr. Kimmel received an emergency call. A sixteen-year-old named Jacob Terrazas needed lifesaving surgery. Dr. Kimmel wanted to help, but how would he get to the hospital—and would it even be safe to go outside during the storm?

The flooding of city streets made roads impassable by car.

The hospital sent two firemen to Dr. Kimmel's house. Using both a truck and a canoe, depending on the water's depth, the team led the doctor to the hospital. "I felt that these guys knew what they were doing, so I didn't worry about myself at all the whole time," he says. Dr. Kimmel walked the last mile to the hospital in waist-deep water. His **dedication** paid off. He arrived just in time to help Jacob.

> **❝**Somebody had to take care of this young man, and so I thought, well, if I can do it, I certainly should.**❞**
>
> –Dr. Stephen Kimmel

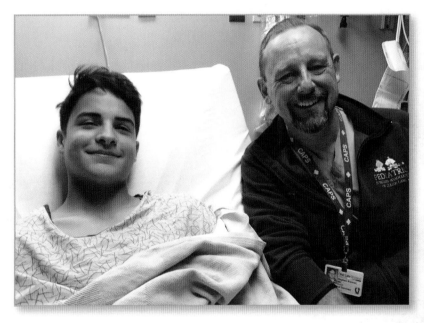

Dr. Stephen Kimmel with his patient, Jacob Terrazas

Hurricane Harvey shut down over sixteen hospitals in the Houston area. More than 1,000 patients had to be moved to other locations.

An emergency vehicle plows through several feet of water.

13

Tragedy

Not everyone was as lucky as Jacob. In nearby Beaumont, Texas, a mother and her three-year-old daughter were driving down a highway to escape the storm. The water rose quickly around their car. Clutching her child, the terrified mother decided to get out of the car to escape to drier ground. Suddenly, a wave of water swept them away.

Flooding in Beaumont, a town about 85 miles (137 km) east of Houston

The mother and child had drifted for nearly half a mile (0.8 km) when a police boat spotted them. The child was clinging to her mother's chest. Two divers swam to the pair and pulled them from the water. The child was safe because the mother had kept her daughter's head above water. Sadly, it was too late for the mother, who had drowned before the rescuers could reach her. Officer Carol Riley said the mom had "absolutely saved the child's life."

Police patrolled the floodwaters with specially trained swimmers and divers to help rescue victims.

At least 100 people were killed as a result of Hurricane Harvey.

The Coast Guard

Many more people in Texas might have died, had it not been for the US Coast Guard. Over 2,000 guardsmen and guardswomen traveled from all over the country to help rescue people stranded by Hurricane Harvey. Using helicopters specially built to travel through storms, the rescuers flew to flooded homes.

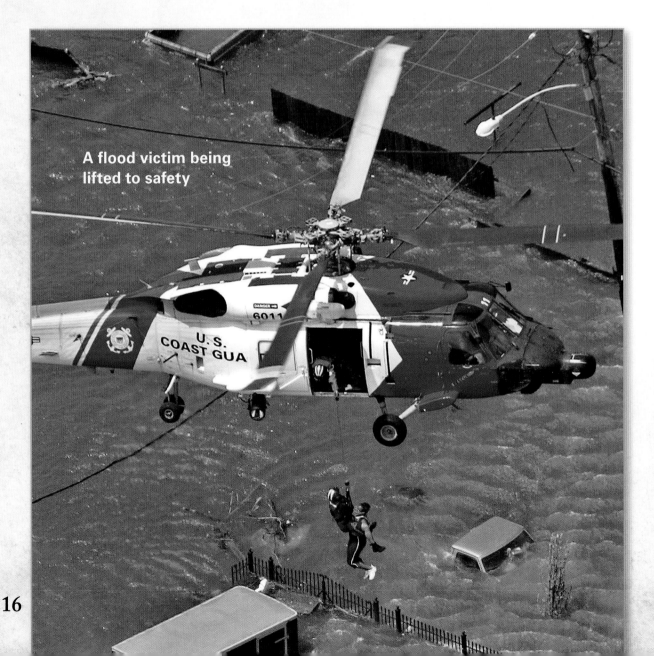

A flood victim being lifted to safety

One rescue **mission** put Coast Guard pilot Lt. Neil Romans in a very difficult spot. His helicopter was low on fuel when he learned of a young woman trapped in a flooded house. Neil needed to refuel the helicopter, but he and his crew refused to **abandon** the woman. Spotting the woman's house, they swooped down and **hovered** in the air. The chopper had to be careful not to hit trees, telephone poles, and wires. Then they lifted the woman to safety. "This is what we signed up for," said rescue swimmer Nick Gardner.

Proud Coast Guardsmen, including Lt. Neil Romans (second from left) and Nick Gardner (far right) stand in front of their helicopter.

The Coast Guard rescued over 11,000 people during Hurricane Harvey. It was their biggest disaster response to date.

66 I was really surprised . . . how many people were still stranded. It was pretty shocking. **99**

–Coast Guard rescue swimmer Nick Gardner

Cajun Navy

In addition to the Coast Guard and police, everyday people risked their safety to help those in need. One group was known as the **Cajun** Navy. Its members had traveled from neighboring Louisiana with their rescue supplies, including small boats. Many had suffered during Hurricane Katrina and wanted to give back to the Texans who had helped them.

Members of the Cajun Navy and volunteers from across the country used their own boats to help rescue people.

Hurricane Katrina flooded New Orleans—the biggest city in Louisiana—in 2005. Many people left New Orleans afterward and settled in Houston, only to be hit by Hurricane Harvey twelve years later.

❝I was young during Katrina, and I know how it feels to lose everything. So being able to help others going through this situation that I have experienced, there's no way—no way—I could pass up helping.❞

–Jordy Bloodsworth, Cajun Navy

Wilma Ellis, a 73-year-old Texan, was floating face-down in the water when Cajun Navy **volunteer** Joshua Lincoln spotted her. Joshua pulled Wilma from the water and noticed she wasn't breathing. He immediately began **resuscitating** her, saving her life. "Just the way we were brought up," said Todd Gaspard, another Cajun Navy volunteer. "You help your neighbor."

Members of the Cajun Navy helping an elderly woman

Rescuing Animals

It wasn't just humans who required help during Hurricane Harvey. Animals needed a hand, too. One dog was tied to a telephone pole and left behind when the storm slammed Texas. Photographer Ruaridh Connellan spotted the dog and ran through knee-deep water to free her. He named the little dog Lucky. "There is no doubt in my mind, if I didn't unleash Lucky from the tree, she would have drowned," said Ruaridh.

The Coast Guard rescued over one thousand pets during Hurricane Harvey.

A concerned volunteer carries a frightened dog to safety.

Other animals did whatever they could to survive the storm. A female hawk flew into a taxicab for safety! The bird entered an open window in the car and then refused to leave. William Bruso, a kindhearted cabdriver, took the bird home. After the storm, he found a team of wildlife experts to care for her. Harvey the hawk, named for the storm, quickly recovered and was later released back into the wild.

Harvey is a kind of bird of prey called a Cooper's hawk.

Harvey was released at Oak Point Park, outside Houston.

66 People lost their lives during Harvey. This hawk survived. . . . and I'm glad for that. 99

–William Bruso, cabdriver in Houston

No Shelter

As storm water from Hurricane Harvey spilled into homes across southeastern Texas, many people needed a safe place to stay. The government set up shelters where people could get food and sleep. Unfortunately, the shelters soon ran out of beds. Some visitors had to sleep on cardboard boxes instead of mattresses.

During the hurricane, over ten thousand people crammed into the George R. Brown Convention Center in downtown Houston.

Many people lost power during Hurricane Harvey. At one point, over 300,000 Houston homes had no electricity because of the storm.

One Houston business owner personally helped with the housing crisis. Jim McIngvale, known as "Mattress Mack," turned his furniture stores into community shelters. Jim sent out delivery trucks to rescue people and bring them to his stores. Then, Jim gave his neighbors warm food and comfortable beds where they could sleep.

Jim McIngvale's own home was flooded during the storm. His neighbors were so impressed by his kind actions that they asked for an official "Mattress Mack Day" in Houston.

Jim "Mattress Mack" McIngvale

66 For what looks like 100 miles is just water, water, water everywhere. It's really stressing to the community, but we're all positive we're going to come together. 99

–Jim McIngvale

Devastating Damage

After Hurricane Harvey ended, Texans began to survey the horrible damage left behind. According to one estimate, as many as 40,000 Houston homes were destroyed. Over one million cars were ruined. More than 75 Houston schools had to be closed. Hurricane Harvey also wrecked water treatment plants, leaving many people without clean water to drink.

Many people lost their homes during the storm, including most of their belongings.

As Harvey **survivor** Lathan Oliver looked at his soaked belongings sitting on a curb, he told a reporter, "As you can see, it's a total waste." However, Lathan knew things could have been far worse for him and his close neighbors. "We didn't lose a life in here. Everyone made it out alive."

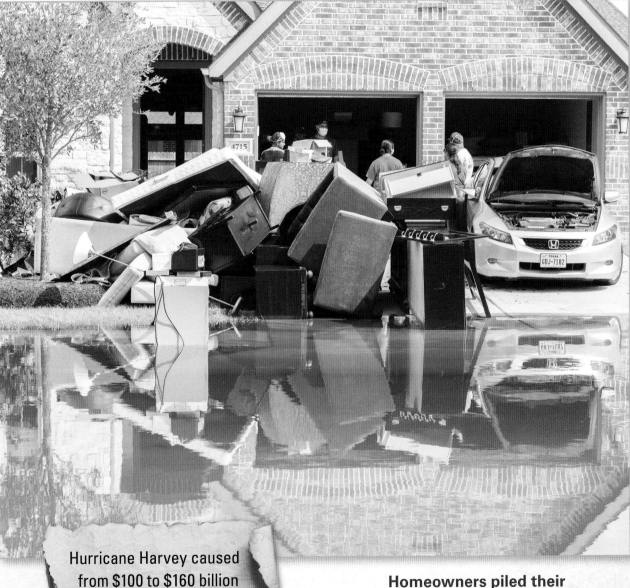

Hurricane Harvey caused from $100 to $160 billion in property damage.

Homeowners piled their ruined, soaked belongings on the street.

Cleaning Up

Cleaning up after Hurricane Harvey took a great deal of work. The storm left millions of tons of garbage on the streets. Badly damaged houses and buildings had to be torn down and rebuilt. "This is going to be a massive, massive cleanup process," said Texas Governor Greg Abbott.

Hurricane Harvey left behind a lot of work for the people of Texas.

To help Texans, the US government sent over 500 people to assist with the effort. Thousands of Texas residents also received money from the government to fix their homes. However, the people hit by the storm know that money alone won't solve the problems left by the deadly hurricane. It will take years and years of hard work.

Government workers load supplies onto a helicopter to help flood victims.

A federal **agency** called FEMA—or the Federal Emergency Management Agency—has a team of specially trained workers to help areas like Houston recover from **disasters**.

Profiles

Many people showed great courage and compassion during Hurricane Harvey. Here are four of them:

Andrea Smith went into labor when Hurricane Harvey hit.

- Was in her Houston home as waters rose
- Prepared to deliver her baby at home when she couldn't reach emergency help
- Grabbed on to the human chain made by her neighbors to reach a rescue truck
- Safely delivered her baby in a hospital, hours later

Dr. Stephen Kimmel performed emergency surgery during Hurricane Harvey.

- Was in his flooded home when he found out that a young man needed lifesaving surgery
- Paddled a canoe toward the hospital
- Walked through waist-deep water
- Performed successful surgery on the young man, saving his life

Lt. Neil Romans is a member of the US Coast Guard, which saved victims from the floods during Hurricane Harvey.

- Flew a special helicopter into the storm
- Lifted victims out of floodwaters, careful to avoid trees and power lines
- Risked his own safety to save a stranded woman even though his own helicopter's fuel was low
- Returned to the floodwaters to help more people

Jim McIngvale, a Houston resident and business owner, helped his community by giving his neighbors shelter during Harvey.

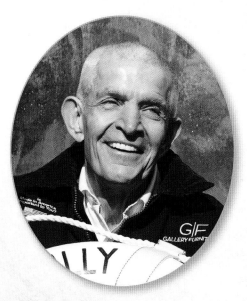

- Was flooded out of his home during the storm
- Sent delivery trucks to rescue strangers from the flood
- Opened up his stores to victims
- Provided victims with a safe place to rest and sleep

Glossary

abandon (uh-BAN-duhn) to leave alone and uncared for

agency (AY-juhn-see) an organization that performs a service for people

Cajun (KAY-juhn) a person from Louisiana whose ancestors are French Canadian

climate change (KLYE-mit CHAYNJ) environmental changes due to the buildup of greenhouse gases that trap the sun's heat in Earth's atmosphere

Coast Guard (KOHST GARD) a branch of the military that protects a nation's coastlines and comes to the aid of boats and ships in trouble

dedication (ded-uh-KAY-shuhn) to give a lot of time and energy to something

disasters (duh-ZASS-turz) events that cause terrible destruction

evacuate (ee-VAK-yoo-ate) to leave a dangerous place

frantically (FRAN-tik-lee) very nervously

hovered (HUHV-urd) floated in place in the air

hurricane (HUR-uh-kane) a storm with very high winds and heavy rain

meteorologists (mee-tee-ur-OL-oh-jists) scientists who study and predict the weather

mission (MISH-uhn) a certain job or task to be performed

reservoirs (REZ-ur-vwarz) natural or artificial lakes for storing water

resuscitating (ri-SUHS-i-teyt-ing) bringing back to life

surgeon (SURH-juhn) a doctor who performs operations

survivor (sur-VYE-vur) a person who lived through a disaster

torrential (tuh-REN-shul) coming in a large, fast stream

transformed (transs-FORMD) changed into something else

tropical wave (TROP-uh-kuhl WAVE) a circular storm that forms over the ocean, with heavy rains and winds between 39 and 73 miles per hour (63 and 117 kph)

volunteer (vol-uhn-TIHR) a person who does a job without pay, in order to help others

water vapor (WAW-tur VAY-pur) water that has changed into a gas; water vapor rises and spreads out through the air

Bibliography

Carroll, Susan. "Nature Ruled, Man Reacted. Hurricane Harvey Was Houston's Reckoning." *Houston Chronicle* (Dec. 9, 2017).

Friedman, Lisa, and John Schwartz. "How Hurricane Harvey Became So Destructive." *The New York Times* (Aug. 28, 2017).

Kimmelman, Michael. "Lessons from Hurricane Harvey: Houston's Struggle Is America's Tale." *The New York Times* (Nov. 11, 2017).

Read More

Aronin, Miriam. *Mangled by a Hurricane! (Disaster Survivors).* New York: Bearport (2010).

Hojem, Benjamin. *Hurricanes: Weathering the Storm (All Aboard Science Reader).* New York: Grosset & Dunlap (2010).

Learn More Online

To learn more about Hurricane Harvey, visit
www.bearportpublishing.com/CodeRed

Index

About the Author

Kevin Blake lives in Providence, Rhode Island, with his wife, Melissa, his son, Sam, and his daughter, Ilana. He has written many nonfiction books for kids.